Living on Your Own

by Stuart Schwartz and Craig Conley

Content Consultant:
Robert J. Miller, Ph.D.
Associate Professor
Mankato State University

CAPSTONE
HIGH/LOW BOOKS
an imprint of Capstone Press

C A P S T O N E   P R E S S

818 North Willow Street • Mankato, MN 56001
http://www.capstone-press.com

Library of Congress Cataloging-in-Publication Data
Schwartz, Stuart, 1945-
    Living on your own/by Stuart Schwartz and Craig Conley
    p. cm. -- (Life skills)
    Includes bibliographical references and index.
    Summary: Explains the fundamental steps toward achieving personal and financial
independence.
    ISBN 1-56065-719-7
    1. Life skills--Juvenile literature. 2. Satisfaction--Juvenile literature. 3. Finance,
Personal--Juvenile literature. [1. Life skills.] I. Conley, Craig, 1965- . II. Title.
III. Series: Schwartz, Stuart, 1945- Life skills.
HQ2037.S28 1998
646.7--dc21   97-51297
                                          CIP
                                          AC

Photo credits:
All photos by Dede Smith Photography

Table of Contents

Chapter 1

Choices and Responsibility

People who live on their own have many responsibilities. They must take care of themselves. They must make many choices.

People who live on their own must earn money to pay expenses. They must pay rent every month. They also must buy food, clothing, and household items.

People who live on their own set goals for themselves. A goal is an objective that a person tries to accomplish. For example, a worker's goal is to buy a car. The worker puts money into the bank each month. The worker reaches the goal by saving money.

Most people enjoy living on their own. They like learning new skills.

People who live on their own have many responsibilities.

Chapter 2

Finding a Job

Most people who live on their own need jobs. They must earn money to pay their bills and buy food and clothing.

People look for jobs that interest them. They can find jobs in many places. Many companies list job openings in newspapers. Some companies list job openings on the Internet. Employment agencies help people find jobs.

Employers ask applicants to fill out applications. An employer is a person or company that hires and pays workers. An applicant is a person who applies for a job. Applications ask for information about people's job skills and work experience. Employers look at applications to choose people who are qualified for jobs.

Employers ask qualified applicants to attend interviews. An interview is a meeting between employers and applicants. Employers ask about applicants' job skills and experience. Applicants often send thank-you letters to employers after interviews. This shows that applicants want the jobs.

People who live on their own need to find jobs.

[Chapter 3]

Being a Responsible Worker

Responsible workers have good work habits. They arrive at work on time. They miss work only when they are ill or they take earned vacation time. Responsible workers follow the rules of the workplace. They work hard every day. They work well with others.

Employers value workers with good work habits. For example, a clerk in a picture frame store is friendly and helpful to customers. She works hard and does not waste time. She has good work habits. Her employer values her work.

Responsible workers try to get along with co-workers. They help each other finish their jobs. For example, a factory worker may help a co-worker lift a heavy box. An office worker may help another worker use a computer. Employers value workers who can work well with each other.

Responsible workers work well with others.

BUS
STOP

ROUTES

8

REGIONAL TRANSIT SYSTEM

Chapter 4

Finding a Place to Live

People who live on their own choose places to live. They should consider several things when choosing a place to live.

People should figure out how much money they can spend on rent. They should know the amount of money they earn in one month. Then they should add up all their expenses. This is the amount they will pay for food, clothing, and other goods and services. People should subtract expenses from the amount they earn. Then they can see how much is left to spend on rent.

People should also consider what kind of housing they want. People can rent apartments or houses. People who plan to live in one area for a long time may want to buy a house or apartment.

People also must decide where to live. They must consider how far to live from work. People without cars may look for housing near bus stops or subway stations. Finding a safe neighborhood to live in is also important.

People without cars may look for housing near bus stops or subway stations.

Chapter 5

Being Financially Responsible

People who live on their own must be careful with the money they earn. Responsible people spend and save money wisely.

Responsible people keep track of their money. They know how much money they earn each month. They know what their monthly expenses are. They know how much they have left over after paying bills.

Responsible people pay bills on time. People who pay bills on time earn good credit. People who have good credit can get loans for houses, cars, and other big purchases. People who have bad credit often have trouble getting loans.

Responsible people put money from each paycheck into savings accounts. They save money for items they want. They also save money for emergencies. An emergency is an unexpected situation.

Responsible people keep track of their money.

Chapter 6

Daily Planning

People who live on their own plan their daily activities. Planning helps people use their time wisely. It helps them complete tasks.

Some people plan their time by making lists. They list everything they must do each day. They decide how important each activity is. They put the most important activities at the top of the list. This helps them get the most important things done first.

For example, a person makes a list of things to do in one day. The person puts paying bills first on the list. Going to the supermarket is second on the list. Walking the dog is third. Washing clothes is fourth.

Lists can help people organize their time. Lists help people know exactly which tasks to do each day. People who finish their tasks may have free time. They can spend free time doing things they enjoy.

Many people who live on their own plan their daily activities.

Chapter 7

Staying Healthy

Responsible people take steps to stay healthy. They know the benefits of healthy bodies.

Healthy people eat balanced diets. A diet is the kinds of food a person usually eats. A balanced diet includes breads, fruits and vegetables, dairy products, and meat. Eating a balanced diet provides nutrients that people need to stay strong and healthy.

Responsible people know they can benefit from daily exercise. Exercise helps build stronger bodies. People can take part in many types of exercise. Some people go on long walks or bike rides. Others use workout equipment at gyms. Some people join sports teams.

Getting enough sleep is also important. Most people need seven or eight hours of sleep each night. People who sleep well wake up ready to do their best.

A balanced diet includes fruits and vegetables.

Chapter 8

Personal Hygiene

Responsible people use good hygiene. Hygiene is all the actions a person takes to be clean. Good hygiene leads to good health.

Good hygiene includes bathing or showering regularly. It also includes keeping hair clean and combed. Washing clothes is also part of good hygiene.

Brushing teeth at least twice a day is important. Brushing teeth keeps teeth from rotting. It also prevents bad breath.

Some people do not have good hygiene. This can cause problems for them at work. Most employers require that workers have good hygiene. For example, a salesperson in a clothing store does not bathe or shower. The salesperson does not smell clean. Customers notice the smell. They may complain to the store owner. Or they may not shop at the store ever again.

Washing clothes is one part of good hygiene.

Chapter 9

Doing Chores

People who live on their own must do chores at home. Chores are daily or weekly household tasks. Responsible people keep up with their chores.

Many people do certain chores every day. They wash their dishes. They make their beds.

People do other chores once or twice per week. They may wait to do these chores on weekends or on their days off from work. They may wash clothes every Saturday. They may vacuum the carpet every Wednesday. They may take out the garbage every Monday and Thursday.

Roommates share chores. A roommate is a person who shares living space with another person. Roommates divide the chores. Each roommate does an equal amount of work.

People who live on their own must do chores at home.

[Chapter 10]

Making Friends

People who live on their own benefit from making friends. They can call friends if they are lonely. They go to movies or out to dinner with friends. Friends can help them get through hard times.

People can make new friends in many places. People can make new friends at work. They can make friends at churches or schools.

Friends often share common interests. For example, a pilot likes to build things. The pilot may take a community education class to learn carpentry. The pilot enjoys being with others who like carpentry. The pilot makes new friends in the class.

People who value friendships are kind to their friends. They listen to their friends' problems. They do not say bad things about them to others. They look for friends who also value friendships. They know that good friendships can improve their lives.

People can meet new friends at work.

Chapter 11

Free Time

People who live on their own choose how to spend their free time. They may use free time to do chores or to do things they enjoy. Many people spend free time with friends.

People who live on their own can have more free time if they are organized. Organized people take care of chores right away. They make their beds as soon as they wake up. They wash dishes after every meal.

People spend their free time doing things they enjoy. Some may like to read or watch television. Some enjoy shopping or going to movies. Many people spend their free time outdoors. Some people work on their hobbies. Sewing, painting, and woodworking are some examples of hobbies.

Some people like to shop in their free time.

[Chapter 12]

Living on Your Own

Living on your own can be exciting. It can also be hard work. You must be willing to take responsibility for yourself. You must make good choices.

You are responsible for earning money to pay your bills. You must find a job and be a responsible worker.

Remember to exercise regularly and eat a balanced diet. Exercise and a good diet will help you stay healthy. Practice good personal hygiene.

Being organized can help you meet your responsibilities. It can help you finish your chores. You will have more free time. You can spend more time with friends.

Living on your own can help you grow. You know that you can take care of yourself.

Being organized can help you meet your responsibilities.

Words to Know

chore (CHOR)—a daily or weekly household task

employment agency (em-PLOI-muhnt AY-juhn-see)—a business that helps people find jobs

goal (GOHL)—an objective that people try to accomplish

hygiene (HYE-jeen)—all the actions a person takes to be clean

interview (IN-tur-vyoo)—a meeting between employers and applicants

responsibility (ri-spon-suh-BIL-uh-tee)—something that must be done

responsible (ri-SPON-suh-buhl)—dependable

roommate (ROOM-mate)—a person who shares living space with another person

To Learn More

Milios, Rita. *Discovering How to Make Good Choices*. New York: Rosen Publishing Group, 1992.

Milios, Rita. *Independent Living*. New York: Rosen Publishing Group, 1992.

Sonbuchner, Gail. *Help Yourself: How to Take Advantage of Your Learning Styles*. New York: New Readers Press, 1991.

Useful Addresses

Adult Education/Training Information Service
325 Queens Avenue
London, Ontario N6B 1X2
Canada

National School to Work Information and Learning Center
400 Virginia Avenue SW, Room 210
Washington, DC 20024

National Center on Adult Literacy
University of Pennsylvania
3910 Chestnut Street
Philadelphia, PA 19104

Internet Sites

America's Job Bank
http://www.ajb.dni.us/

Career Search
http://learningedge.sympatico.ca/
  careersearch/index.html

**Independent Living Skills Network-
  U.S.A. and Canada**
http://www.nas.com/~ilpf/Everett.htm

Information on Finding a Job
http://www4.usnews.com/usnews/edu/
  beyond/bccooh1.htm

Self-Assessment
http://www.bsu.edu/careers/selfases.html

Index